From Wallflower Blues
to Red Hot Dancing Shoes

A Goddess Guide to Joyful Living
and Fabulous Self-Care

Sharron Phillips

WOW NOW Press
New York

This book contains the ideas and opinions of the author. The recommendations made in this book are not meant to replace professional consultation with physicians, mental health professionals, or clergy. In the event you use any of the ideas and opinions in this book for yourself, the author and publisher assume no responsibility or liability.

WOW NOW Press
P.O. Box 486
Chester, New York 10918

ISBN 0-9785373-1-9
Library of Congress number 2007935001

Dedication

With great appreciation to
all of my husbands.
You each guided me to take
better and better care of
myself.

I am grateful.

Contents

Acknowledgments

My gratitude goes out to my book coach, Kathy Gulrich, who held my hand in the beginning stages of formulating the idea and plan.

I enlisted readers to help guide me and I appreciate their willingness and feedback. Thank you to Connie Wehmeyer, Jan Connell, Melissa Ochs, Tammy Prince, Gail Miller, and Lynn Chase.

There was steady encouragement from my Mastermind group and they kept me accountable. You know who you are Al, Connie, and Margie!

My editor has been a gift from the goddesses. Thank you, Lauren Manoy, for coming into my life. I am inspired to continue writing to reap the benefits of being associated with you professionally.

And a final "tip of the hat" to my beloved, Perry Harris, who blazed the trail in our house by publishing his first book, *Wake Up Through Dreaming*.

Introduction

Some of us grow up instinctively knowing how to nurture ourselves because of amazing role models in our early years. Some of us need to learn later in life. Based on my life experience, I'd like to plant seeds for women who are interested in learning how to improve their own self-care and nurturing skills.

Embrace a *self-ish* attitude. This is different from a selfish attitude. A dictionary definition of selfish is "concerned chiefly or only with oneself."[1] I would like to define self-ish as a willingness to be aware of how important conscious self-care is. The benefits of conscious self-care can lead to a wholesome, integrated, healthy human being who is capable of contribution and fulfilled living through having developed clarity, energy, vision, and authenticity.

Stay current with what works in your life. An exercise routine you used ten years ago may need to be modified. You may need to make new friends. You may need to learn how to start saying no to requests from friends, family, clubs, and school functions. You may need to block out part of a day each week to create time for you. You may need to learn how to make requests. You are constantly evolving, so what works at one time in your life may not work at another time. Develop flexibility.

Start now. No more excuses. Let go of feeling that you need to be perfect, that you have to take care of everyone else before you can think about you, that you have to say "yes" when you'd rather say "no," that you have no time for yourself. You have a lifetime of choices, and you get to make those choices every day. Begin to tailor your choices so that you are included.

How to Use this Book

I would like to invite you to make this a guidebook and workbook that you feel comfortable with. Get the full value out of it —make notes to yourself, dog-ear the pages—squeeze the juice out of the pages. Buy small "Post It" notes in a variety of colors to mark pages and create a rainbow as you proceed. Celebrate your action steps with notations and doodles about your successes, your mistakes, steps forward/backward/sideways, confusions, and your discoveries. Write your answers, responses, or ponderings right in the book if you want to. This might be a real challenge for some of you. Many of us were taught not to write in a book. I remember the first time I saw a very well-used book with notations, underlining, and turned-over page corners. I was attending a workshop with Gary Zukav and a woman approached him with his book, *The Seat of the Soul* in her hand. At first I felt an element of shock and wonder that someone could have "attacked" the book in this way. But then what I noticed was the enthusiasm, dedication, and value that the owner had for the book's material. I could feel that she was using the book lovingly as a resource for her learning and integration of the subject matter. I vowed that I would try to love a book in that way if the contents were as compelling for me as for the woman in the example above.

I suggest that you read through the whole book first to get the flavor of the subject matter. Then, feel free to flip from section to section. See what interests you at the moment and read that section.

About Small Action Steps

At the end of each chapter I have listed some suggested action steps. There is untold power in small action steps! Please be willing to create and follow the small action step model. Perhaps you have more experience with thinking bigger about how to carry out a plan. "I want it ALL, and I want it NOW!" Is this a familiar pattern in your approaches to life goals?

What can happen is overwhelm and confusion. Many times when we can find success in the very small steps toward a goal or dream or project, we are subconsciously empowered to continue with the next part. Try to create action steps for a new idea, activity, or experiment in very doable, understandable, and easy-to-complete tasks. Why not enjoy the process and stay away from crippling timetables and expectations?

Who are you and what are you letting go of? Bravo for all that you learn about yourself!

Also, notice that I often suggest an action step that involves sharing material with a friend. The purpose of speaking about your new idea and action step is that simply by inviting another person to witness and participate in your journey you are making a commitment to following through. P.S. There is a difference between saying to someone, "I should get started" and " Here is my next step that I am taking toward my goal." Notice the wishful thinking and procrastination of the first statement. Feel the energy in the second stated intention.

Psychological
Self-Care

Stop judging yourself

Start celebrating **mistakes**

Stay curious

Learn **to delegate**

Discover **your limiting beliefs**

Be generous **by**
giving yourself permission

Evaluate **what**
perfectionism does for you

Judgment

She really shouldn't be wearing that...He must eat junk food continually to be that large...They could use a lesson in manners...That's the dumbest idea I've ever heard....

A dictionary definition of judgmental is, "Inclined to make judgments, esp. moral or personal ones."[2]

Letting Go

I am going to ask you to consider letting go of some of your judgmental tendencies. We all judge. Some of us judge more than others. Some of us judge loudly, and some of us judge quietly. Living each day making judgments, both verbal and mental, of yourself and those around you, takes a lot of energy. You will see that it is exhausting work once you pay attention to how much time and effort you put into being a judge. By being kinder to yourself and others, you will feel more relaxed and vibrant. This is positive self-care and leaves extra time and energy for you to devote to being your wonderful self.

P.S. This is another of those lifelong learning experiences, so be patient. Keep moving forward with small steps, and you will see a difference in your quality of life.

See More than Just Black and White

I grew up trained to think and live in black and white. There was right and wrong, good and bad, true and false, and nothing in between. I knew how to judge myself and everyone else: driving styles, dress styles, hairstyles, behavior. I was sure I knew the right way and could point my finger knowingly when someone or something did not follow the rules. I was very busy worrying about what everyone else was doing and happy to point out any deviation from the norm. I did my best to understand all the rules around me, and if I didn't live up to them, I considered myself a failure.

Enjoy the Grace of Grey Areas

The gift of accepting that there are grey areas, the areas between black and white, is that I have become much more relaxed and comfortable. Getting used to the idea of grey areas has freed me up tremendously. I can give myself permission to see everything in black or white or grey. It's okay to acknowledge that there are fuzzy areas of life. It is a key to my self-care.

We're all doing the best we can—even when it doesn't look that way.

Let go of judging yourself and the people around you. Be patient with yourself. Be gentle with yourself.

Consider being open to knowing that there are always things you may not know or have experience with. Why judge? Somehow life feels less harsh, and you may find yourself becoming more open to feeling less pressured to pronounce judgment.

You Can't Change Other People

I know this one very well! Isn't this one of the biggest jobs in the world? And isn't this the least satisfying and successful job? Most of us fall into the trap of believing that we can get someone to change a behavior or thought if we try hard enough. A classic learning opportunity for me was the time I believed that I could get someone to stop smoking who wasn't ready to want it for himself. Agony!

Step back and recall if you have had success in changing someone who you judged as being wrong about something. Realize that the only person you can change is yourself. That's a big enough task!

Get used to change.

Change is a constant in Nature and in Life. The better you flow with change, the better you can flow in your life. Make friends with change. Changes bring opportunities to learn more about who you are.

Welcome change!

Small Action Steps

1. Listen to what you say. Do you include "should," "could," and "ought to" frequently in talking and thinking about other people and about yourself? This could be a way to spot a judgment easily.

2. How do you feel when someone judges you?

3. If you are learning to be accepting of yourself, what are the areas that you would like to start with?

4. Have a conversation with a friend about what judgments you each use in your personal lives.

Teamwork

Going solo, shouldering every ounce of responsibility that you can find, is likely to wear you down. Perhaps that's where you are right now…worn out! Give yourself a break.

Create Your Teams

Create teams around you in your home life, personal life, and work life. Learn to enjoy the process of creating a team and working with your hand-picked team. Give yourself permission to benefit from someone else's viewpoint and experience. This may take some getting used to. This may also involve letting go of control. You may wonder what took you so long to implement a team to support you.

We often involve friends to create an informal team when we have a problem we need help with. In difficult times a family can become an emergency-care team. Find and gather experts together to help with a project or problem that needs a solution.

Teamwork in your personal life might look like the following example. I wanted to make a hundred and fifty origami cranes for my wedding. A dear friend of mine knows how to do origami. She offered to help me make the cranes, and we spent about ten hours folding paper together. As well as completing the task, we enjoyed the opportunity to socialize for that time. With our very busy schedules, it was a treat to reconnect with each other. I was grateful that I had accepted her generous offer of time and expertise. Allow yourself to receive help when it is offered!

Brainstorm

Brainstorming is defined in my dictionary as "to engage in or organize shared problem solving."[3] Brainstorming with other people will add value to your life and is an important self-care practice. There's a difference between brainstorming and asking others to make your decisions for you.

For example, I am a member of a Mastermind group. We are a group of four that meets twice a month to keep current on each others' projects and businesses. We listen to each other in turn and offer suggestions that may be helpful. I am continually amazed at the quality of the input I receive from my group and the innovation that they offer me. I am learning to think outside of the box by having joined this team of wildly creative personalities. Ten years ago I would have felt really uncomfortable sitting with them. I would have thought that they had impractical, wacky, pipedream ideas. I have come to appreciate that imaginative approaches can lead to beautiful solutions, and it is fun being a part of the process!

Involve the Family

In a home setting, brainstorming as a family can be just as useful. Everyone has a point of view, and putting all the possibilities on the table is a way to get the best solution; in addition, the process of discussing possibilities helps us keep connected with how we each see the world. This is a wonderful opportunity to share everyone's creative ideas, and even though not every idea will be used, you may take bits and pieces of each idea and arrive at an amazing solution!

Delegate

Do you delegate at home and at work? This aspect of self-care means letting go of doing it all.

Pay Someone Else with Money or Time

If you would rather not do housework, pay someone else to do it, barter, or rearrange house rules so that those chores are at least shared.

I decided that I did not want to learn how to set up a website and am paying someone to do that. I will also be paying someone to maintain the site. I was tempted to take the project on and do it myself. What occurred to me was that I sit at the computer enough as it is and don't want to add more hours to what exists already. It took some time to get to the decision that I made, and I feel like I really took great care of myself by letting go of doing it all.

If you don't know how to delegate, start practicing. Delegating means assigning a task to someone else who is better equipped to complete the task, or who is willing to accept the task and do what needs to be done to complete it. Get used to figuring out what you can do, what you prefer not to do, and what you really don't know how to do.

Make Specific Requests

Communicate with your spouse, family, and friends. Let them know what you would like help with. Ask for help with a specific request for a specific task. Asking with

Example

More helpful: Would you be willing to make dinner on Monday evening?

Less helpful: You never help with meals. I have to do it by myself all the time.

a request will be more effective than demanding that something be done. Make the request specific, doable, and in the moment.

Accept Tasks with Meaning

Minimize the tasks that you dislike and feel responsible for. Spend time reviewing just what needs to be done and with what frequency. Also, spend some time analyzing whether the tasks you have are ones that add value to your life. Do you force yourself to complete some chores that are outdated in your present life? It's okay to rearrange your routine!

Small Action Steps

1. Promise yourself to ask for help when you need it!

2. Create a team for your next project. Who will you invite to join you?

3. Delegate a task at home. Why will this help you?

4.Brainstorm with your family for your next vacation.

5. When someone offers to help you, let them. What will be the benefit of receiving help?

Limiting Beliefs

We each have thoughts and beliefs that we have learned, stored, and accepted. Some of those thoughts and beliefs are limiting beliefs. Limiting beliefs are thoughts that hold us back from achieving our full potential. Many times we are not aware that we have limiting beliefs and are surprised when we unearth them. Most often a limiting belief is best discarded so that you are free to receive more love, money, peace, and happiness into your life.

For example, if in your mind and heart you hold a belief that money is the root of all evil, that money corrupts your integrity, that money means you will lose your friends, then you will likely not attract money to you. Energetically, the limiting beliefs you are holding will keep steering you to sabotage your financial abundance.

You can give yourself a huge gift in the self-care department when you understand what your limiting beliefs are. Negative or limiting beliefs can infiltrate any part of daily life. Where do you find them? How do you dislodge the limiting beliefs that no longer hold value or add to your quality of life? Recognizing and sifting out limiting beliefs will be a boost to your self-care.

Dislodge Limiting Beliefs

The first step to get unstuck from negative and limiting beliefs is paying attention to what you tell yourself. Be aware of the subconscious comments you make to yourself as you encounter both familiar and new situations. Listen to yourself as you speak to people, and train your ear to notice when you are making a negative pronouncement or commenting in negative ways. Watch for clichés that are part of your conversation. You may even be able to identify a voice that sounds like the person where your belief came from. Parents, grandparents, teachers, neighbors, and classmates from school have all been influences in our learning various beliefs.

Question Your Beliefs Regularly

The next step is to take some time and sit with what you have noticed that you say or think that may be a negative or limiting belief. Mull over whether this thought or belief is true for you. Does this belief express who you are today?

Examples of Negative or Limiting Beliefs

I'm not smart enough to learn how to use the computer.

Everyone I date is a loser.

Money is the root of all evil.

I could never speak in front of a group of people.

Men only want sex.

I have to lose 20 pounds before I take dance classes.

If you can't do it right, don't do it at all.

Artists can't make a living.

You have choices to make. Which of those beliefs that you currently hold do you want to keep? What are some new beliefs that express who you are or who you want to become?

From Wallflower Blues to Red Hot Dancing Shoes

I spent many years as a wallflower and did not venture out onto the dance floor. I ached to be in the middle of it all, dancing my heart out. My limiting belief was that I would be "making a spectacle of myself." I would tap my feet and imagine moving my body as I stood on the sidelines. I took a jazz dance class, and my husband at the time had come to walk me home from the dance center. He'd seen the class through a window from the street and told me I resembled a baby elephant as I moved across the dance floor. Voilà! Another limiting belief was born.

Over time, I have discarded those limiting beliefs about my dancing ability. I get up on the dance floor quickly now, and I really relish moving and participating in the joy of dance and music.

Never say "Never!"

Be willing to experiment.
Life is full of surprises.
Not many of us have the
ability to know exactly
what we will and won't do
as circumstances arise.

Small Action Steps

1. What are 5 limiting beliefs you hold?

_____

_____

_____

_____

_____

2. Name one limiting belief that you wish to let go of.

_____

_____

_____

_____

_____

3. Share with a friend your plan to release a limiting belief and request their support.

4. For today, keep an ear open to hear if you speak using a limiting belief.

Giving Yourself Permission

According to my dictionary, permission is to "allow, give consent, authorization, and to afford the opportunity or possibility for."[4] Who hands out the permission slips in your life? Is it your parents, family members, friends, community, social network, your church, your spouse, yourself?

It's okay for you to give yourself permission to take care of yourself so that you are operating on all cylinders. You know what keeps you dynamic, healthy, and fulfilled. If you don't know, make the choice to find out.

Take Responsibility

Understand that you are a part of making your self-care a reality. "I will give myself permission to come home at the end of the week and have an uninterrupted bubble bath for a half hour. My family will know that this is my time to relax." This is very empowering and will not only benefit you. Everyone around you will experience the results of you feeling nurtured. It is likely that your mood will be uplifted, that you will be more playful, relaxed, loving, receptive, motivated, and vibrant.

Allow Yourself to Feel Awkward and Delicious

Many times when I hear women use the phrase "I give myself permission" it is announced as a nurturing challenge. It is a new concept that will be awkward and delicious at the same time—awkward because it is the first time you give yourself permission or because it has been a long time since you have been proactive in giving yourself permission. And then, delicious because there is a grand feeling of empowerment, joy and possibility. It's like you're your own boss, parent, angel. Test it out. Be prepared to feel nervous and uncertain in the beginning. Start giving yourself permission to try something new, to ditch the "to do" list, to treat yourself to some reading time, dancing time, girlfriend time, to getting your needs met, to telling your truth, to be perfectly imperfect, to create and strengthen boundaries, to love yourself.

Small Action Steps

1. Say out loud "I give myself permission."

2. Say out loud "I give myself permission to
____."

3. Have a conversation with a friend about what it means to give yourself permission.

4. What are the benefits of giving yourself permission?

Perfectionism

Let's agree to define perfectionism as having accepted standards that are way beyond reach, feeling a need to behave in "the correct way," feeling overwhelmed and unworthy at the possibility of making a mistake, and being overly defensive when given constructive advice.

I have experience being a perfectionist and have found that there is heartache on that path. There was heartache for me because striving for perfection was stifling, rigid, and uncomfortable. I eventually made peace with the reality that I am a human being and blessed with the opportunity to make mistakes, live through them, and learn from them!

Appreciate the Power of Mistakes

How comfortable are you with making a mistake and appreciating that you have an to opportunity learn and grow from it?

It took me a long time to get comfortable with making and owning up to mistakes. It surprises me that it took me so long to let go and be willing to show up "imperfect," "incorrect," or "discombobulated." I have a friend who remained stifled for years. She was unable to try new ventures because of the fear that her first attempt would not be perfect. What a standard to answer to! Fortunately, she has given herself permission to make mistakes as she moves forward.

Give yourself the gift of trust that the world will not end and that you are going to survive and thrive as you challenge yourself to stretch, grow and flourish in spite of—and because of—mistakes that will come along with your fantastic successes! If you allow yourself to make mistakes, acknowledge them, and celebrate them in the spirit of growth and learning, you may feel a sense of freedom and empowerment. When you stretch yourself to discover your talents, desires, and dreams, remember to leave yourself a healthy margin for mistakes. They're part of the package and will serve you well—sometimes showing you a different and improved answer to a problem, sometimes reminding you that you are a human being, and sometimes creating a funny story to share with your friends! For the most part, mistakes let you know that you need to head in a different direction. Repeating the same mistake over and over may be a message that you're not really paying attention and may require some professional help.

Eleanor's Wisdom

I love this quote I found from Eleanor Roosevelt: *Learn from the mistakes of others. You can't live long enough to make them all yourself.* [5]

Wow! Here's an empowering invitation to relish the beauty of mistakes—the ones we each make and the ones others make.

Small Action Steps

1. Celebrate a mistake you have made by telling a friend about it.

2. Think of a mistake you have made. What was the gift of that mistake?

3. Who in your life is a role model for learning from and moving forward after making mistakes?

4. Ask your role model how he or she has come to make use of mistakes he or she makes.

Emotional
Self-Care

Create supportive communities

Strengthen **your boundaries**

Evaluate your relationships

Start to feel your feelings

Start telling your truth

Find out **if you are
a people pleaser**

Creating Community

It feels good to belong. It feels good to belong to a group, a community. A dictionary defines community as "a group of people having common interests, similarity, identity, sharing, participation, and fellowship."[6] Don't we all want to share, participate in, and enjoy relationships?

Many women are very busy and surrounded by lots of people, yet they are stuck and feel isolated and lonely. Sometimes we are moving so quickly and involved in so many groups for short periods of time that we do not get the continuity of friendship and communication that we crave. Isn't it strange to realize that you can be in contact with lots of people and still feel empty and unable to create a relationship?

Design Your Own Communities

A solution to this situation could be forming a group or community that will satisfy your need. I have found great comfort, inspiration and continuity in groups that I have joined and also in groups that I have initiated. I belong to a drumming circle and also a chanting community. I enjoy the spirit of each of those groups and get a sense of belonging and pleasure from our activities together. I have co-created a monthly group to watch inspirational films and also an evening each month to dance freestyle with friends at our home. These groups satisfy my needs to share a spiritual connection and an opportunity to dance regularly.

One of my friends was feeling that her life had changed and that her social circle was very limited. After a while she decided to have an annual Girlfriend Evening. She invites her friends to a theme party that she creates, which satisfies her need for creativity, community, and hosting. It is an evening that I have looked forward to each year, and I am slowly developing new friendships within the circle. The theme this year is belly dancing and we will have a professional belly dancer to teach us some basics. I have my coin belt all ready to go!

Be courageous, creative, and curious about what you would like to share with others on a regular basis. Who you would like to include in the group? Have fun establishing links via communities.

Ideas For
A Girlfriend
Evening

Tea party

Campfire and stories

Belly dance instruction

Game night/charades

Spiritual cinema night

Theme costume evening

Small Action Steps

1. What communities do you belong to that are satisfying?

2. What communities do you belong to that no longer serve your needs?

3. Brainstorm with a friend about what kind of a community you would create to add value to your life.

4. Check out the Internet for discussion groups, forums, and communities that may be of interest to you relating to health issues, family situations, or global topics.

5. Look in your local paper to find out what existing communities you may like to visit.

Boundaries

I first learned about boundaries when I was reading Thomas J. Leonard's writings and studying at virtual Coach U. I automatically pictured barbed wire, fence posts, basketball courts, and stone walls. What are your pictures of boundaries? And specifically, what are your ideas about personal boundaries?

Setting and enforcing boundaries can give us the space to allow us to feel our feelings and become better acquainted with ourselves. Think of a tall building or a tall tree. The building needs a strong underground structure as a tall tree needs a large root base to withstand the forces of Nature and time. Boundaries are necessary to help create a strong foundation. You will attract people who are willing to respect what is important to you. You will strengthen your personal foundation so that you can grow your life by starting with a solid base.

Boundaries Are Necessary

What happens when you have no boundaries? It is likely that unless you have boundaries established, your life will be subject to the whims and preferences of anyone around you. Is it okay for someone to physically harm you? Is it okay for someone to be emotionally abusive to you? Is it okay for someone to be overly critical of you? Is it okay for someone to ridicule you? Is it okay for someone to make demands that are unreasonable? Is it okay to be taken for granted? Do you allow someone to jeopardize your vision and dreams?

You are free to choose what is, and what is not, acceptable behavior from the people around you. You will experience a sense of confidence and self-respect by making choices and being clear about choosing only relationships, behaviors, and environments that nurture you. Sometimes we need to add boundaries as we gain experience in the world and discover behaviors that do not serve us.

Clarify Fuzzy Boundaries

When a boundary is not clear, well-defined, and important to you, it is useless. Your self-care is strengthened when you establish to yourself and those around you what is acceptable and unacceptable behavior.

Once you have made a choice, you are then responsible for creating a way to inform people about your wishes. Use clear communication to express your boundaries. If you do not want phone calls after 9 p.m., then you will need to create a boundary and request that family and friends speak to you before 9 p.m. If you choose not to participate in gossiping, then you would need to say that you are not willing to contribute to or listen to gossip when that is part of the conversation and request that the subject matter shift. If you choose to spend a limited amount of time in a conversation with someone, you would let the other person know how much time you are willing to offer.

Some examples of boundaries:

No one may physically abuse me.

No one may use me to whine to.

No one may emotionally abuse me.

No one may take me for granted.

Boundaries can be expansive more than limiting. When you take the time and give yourself permission to be in charge of yourself, you will provide yourself with room to grow and create supportive relationships and environments.

Become an Expert Boundary Maker

Learn to take steps to create and reinforce the boundaries you need. Educate people so they know what is acceptable to you.

As an example, if you have always allowed a neighbor to walk into your house unannounced and have decided that you want to change that behavior, first talk to the neighbor and say that you have a request that she/he not walk into your house without being invited in. Say to the neighbor that it is important to you because you want to have privacy. Tell him/her that starting right now, you need them to knock at the door and wait until you answer the door before they come in. Because you are setting a boundary, you do not need to get involved in a debate or discussion with the neighbor to negotiate. A boundary is non-negotiable. Remember that if a boundary is well defined and important to you, it will be easier to educate others about how to respect your boundary request.

Set Boundaries for Yourself

What about personal boundaries with yourself? One of my personal boundaries with myself is that I do not invite or contribute to gossip in a conversation. I am tempted to at times, and I am not perfect, so there are times when I do gossip. What I notice is that I feel so strongly about refraining from gossiping or listening to gossip that it is very rare that I ignore my boundary. The times that I do slip, I feel a sharp disappointment in my behavior, and that feeling rekindles my commitment to this boundary.

Small Action Steps

1. List 3 boundaries that are important to you.

2. Why are those 3 boundaries important to you?

3. What is a new boundary that you would like to create that will improve your life?

4. Have a conversation with a family member or friend about what boundaries are and why they are important.

Relationships

Let's start by agreeing that loving, healthy relationships feed and nurture us. Loving, healthy relationships need constant attention. To take better care of yourself, commit to finding the time and energy to attract and maintain quality relationships.

Relate with Your Family

Many of us have more than one family for a variety of reasons. We are born into a family; we may create a family by birthing, adopting, or marrying a partner with children; we may gather people together to co-create a new family. Families are dynamic units, and it can be easy to get lost in the mix of traditions, loyalties, interwoven needs, messy boundaries, aging, illness, communication glitches, relocating, and on and on.

Take some time to acknowledge the number and types of families that you are a member of. You may be surprised at the commitments you have accepted in relationships and responsibilities. If you are overwhelmed, take a step back and review exactly how you want to interact with the family groups in your life. If you are feeling a distance that is uncomfortable, perhaps you need to become proactive in refreshing contacts with people who are important to you that you have lost touch with. In my life, I have realized that my nieces and nephews are not consistently at family gatherings as they are becoming independent and live out of the area. I miss knowing who they are becoming and have decided to be proactive in contacting them so that I can remain a part of their lives.

Become an Adult

One way to practice great self-care is to understand that you are an independent adult. I was 40 years old before I viewed myself as an adult and not as a child of my parents. It was a huge realization and almost embarrassing to see that I was still seeking approval from my parents. I was able at that point to give myself permission to be confident about having differing viewpoints, about having made choices that were right for me, and about expressing my feelings. Have you found your independence yet?

Be a Role Model for Your Children

When you create a family and are a parent, your own self-care comes in maintaining time for you and what keeps you vibrant, energized, and healthy. You are a role model for your children, and they will see clearly how you value yourself. Family demands while raising children are enormous. While enjoying the challenges and beauty of guiding children to maturity, remember that they are watching what you do for your own self-care. If you choose martyrdom, then that will be the model they will know best. If you have no working model of a parent practicing self-care in the midst of raising children, look to see to someone else around you as an example for how to pay attention to self-care.

Here are some pointers I have gleaned from women who maintain a sense of self while they are raising a family. They make time for exercise. This doesn't have to be an elaborate or expensive venture. The point is that there is a space in their week for exercise, which keeps their stress levels down, their bodies fit, and sometimes offers a chance to socialize with friends at the same time. They have dates with their spouses. They have close friends. They take a bubble bath at the end of the week. They read. Make a commitment to figuring out what would work for you so that you are nurturing yourself as you parent. Keep it simple so that it is doable.

Relate to Your Friends

Friends are important. Choose friends who are supportive, loving, and concerned about what is best for you. This is a big part of self-care. What kind of friends do you have? Do you share similar values and interests? Are you glad to have those people in your life? If you have people in your life whom you used to consider friends but who don't fit into your life anymore, then get clarity about what needs to happen. Do you need to have a conversation about how someone can be more supportive about what changes you want to make in your life? Will that alter your ability to remain friends? As we learn and grow, we may find that we need to create new friendships and say goodbye to old friendships.

Sadly, I have had to let go of some friendships. Some of those friendships were active because I wanted to fix something for the friend. I came to see that I couldn't fix anything, and it was painful to watch what I considered to be self-destructive behavior. It was not easy, and it was also an important choice for me to make. I gave myself permission to move on and let go. I know that I still have deep and loving feelings for the friends I no longer see. I have taken care of myself by being true to what feeds me and does not drain me.

Relate to Yourself

Here's the biggie: the relationship you have with yourself. There is a lifetime of discovery for you in developing and refining this relationship. Be patient and curious. Be open to loving yourself. Make the mistakes you need to make as you go along in order to move forward, and know that it is part of the process of discovery. The more fully you can appreciate and love who you are, the more fully you will experience your life—your authentic self.

At a workshop I attended, a question was thrown out to the audience: What we are doing to manifest our most magnificent selves? One woman raised her hand and announced that she was planning a ceremony to marry herself. I was thunderstruck at the idea. Somewhere along the way, she had gotten disconnected from herself, but she was ready to love herself, and she was going to celebrate the shift! I immediately understood what she was doing. The ceremony was to be attended by friends and family. She sent out invitations, was wearing a formal dress, writing vows, and was going to have a feast with a cake afterward. How does this strike you? For me, I was energized by the creativity and boldness and statement of love in the occasion that this person had designed.

Learn to Recognize Toxic Love Relationships

There are some fantasy, storybook ideas that we grab onto only to find that they are fantasy, storybook ideas. The "Leave it to Beaver" TV series, "Donna Reed" TV series, knight-in-shining-armor story, and Prince Charming are examples of these stories.

Think back to stories that you read as a child, teen or young adult. Think back to your mother, aunts, grandmothers, godmothers, teachers and remember what you may have heard about meeting the man you will marry.

Why is this unhealthy? Leaping to a storybook happy ending without understanding the mechanics of real time relationships that are involved to get there, is bound to be confusing, frustrating, and in some cases, potentially dangerous because of emotional and/or physical abuse resulting from naivete.

Sometimes, when we are not loving ourselves fully and when our personal development is needing attention, we experience toxic love relationships. This happens to many of us. In learning about who we are and how love relationships develop, we may choose challenging and unfulfilling partners. We experiment, flounder, and live in a state of denial and confusion until we learn to recognize what we want in a loving, nurturing, fulfilling relationship. How many discussions about relationship skills have you had with parents, teachers or other adults?

It could be that the experience you have is an indicator. Many times we partner with people who will mirror the places where we need to grow. Perhaps, in order to create a more fulfilling love relationship, you will need to create stronger boundaries, learn to communicate clearly, learn how to navigate conflict resolution with integrity and grace, understand your feelings and needs, and develop a higher level of self-worth.

What kind of ceremony would you design to honor loving yourself?

Grow to love yourself and love to grow yourself. The benefits are priceless and the quality of your love relationships will be off the charts.

Small Action Steps

1. Review your relationships with your friends. Which are the friends you want to keep and which are the friends you may need to let go of?

2. Plan a date night with your spouse or partner. What are some ideas for fun things to do together?

3. Imagine what it would be like to marry yourself. Describe the event.

4. Write down what is important to you in a friendship.

_____

_____

_____

_____

_____

_____

5. How many families, groups, circles, communities are you a member of, and do they all hold meaning for you? If they don't, what can you do to improve your time spent interacting in those situations? Do you need to move away from involvement in any of those groups?

Identifying Feelings

Your feelings are worthwhile and valuable tools that guide you. Taking good care of yourself by knowing how you feel is high on the list of priorities for self-care, in my opinion. It may sound easy to know how you feel and what you feel. I have found the practice of moving toward better skills in identifying and verbalizing feelings to be grueling, exciting, fulfilling, and awkward. I realize that this exercise is critical to my well-being, and so I continue to practice. Please consider the advantages you may gain by coming to grips with your feelings and being able to identify and communicate those feelings. You can expect less confusion, more clarity, increased general health and well-being, more effective communication, more self awareness, and peace of mind.

Express Your Feelings

There are many women, myself included, who have spent a lifetime stuffing feelings away, glossing over situations we may not understand, and then moving on to care for someone else's needs or desires. In the aftermath, we are left with unmet needs, confusion, dissatisfaction, and frustration. Another frequent situation is avoiding a conflict by ignoring what we are feeling at the time. This can lead to poor negotiation skills and compromise in matters that affect us. Of course, there are many more scenarios, and I'm sure you can add to the list.

We are human beings, and human beings are built to experience emotions, feelings. A feeling puts us in touch with the human experience. The range of feelings is vast and wide. It is liberating to know that your feelings do not define you; they are part of your experience.

Your Feelings Affect Your Health

Paying attention to recognizing your feelings, feeling your feelings, and letting them go is likely to keep your body in a better state of health. Not acknowledging your feelings, fighting your feelings, or hanging on to empty, outdated feelings can create discomfort and pain in your physical being.

In some traditional Eastern medicines, it is thought that back pain is related to emotional health. I've had my own share of back pain and the resulting immobility. I still remember picturing myself in a wheelchair for the rest of my life, and that was sobering. I would say that there was a hefty element of emotional dis-ease directly related to not acknowledging or verbalizing my feelings that built up and contributed to my back condition. I am pleased to report that I have been pain-free for many years now. The reward for getting in touch with your feelings may lead to a dramatic improvement in your health.

Recognize the Physical Sensation of a Feeling

As I venture forward, acknowledging and feeling my feelings, I tune in to the signals in my body that tell me how I am experiencing the feeling physically. I am finding that frequently when I am opening to feelings that involve communicating/being heard/stating a request, my throat aches and my jaw feels tight. There is a sense of ancient frustration that I can associate with the ache and tightness. The uncomfortable body sensations in my throat and jaw are reminders of the times I was really at a loss to even imagine a way to express my emotions. How many times did I shy away from saying what I wanted to say, from asking for something I wanted, from contributing a new idea, from asking a question?

It is difficult to juggle the sensation of physical discomfort and the act of speaking about the feeling if you are with another person. I know that unless I follow through with experiencing both parts, I will remain numb, frozen, and unfulfilled. What helps me is to remember to slow down and give myself the space I need to pay attention to the physical sensations that result from feelings that arise. With each experience and opportunity to practice feeling a feeling, I am more confident and skilled. I can recommend the adventure of getting in touch with recognizing, naming, and owning your feelings.

Other physical sensations directly related to feelings could include nausea, a rapid heart rate, a sinking feeling in the stomach, "butterflies" in the stomach, backache, neck ache, headache, dizziness, light-headedness, heartache, or a dry mouth.

Stop Exploding

Many women spend their lives avoiding their feelings and then don't know how to recognize them because the feelings have been shelved and hidden for so long. In my experience, I know that feeling and expressing feelings was frightening because I bottled them up until they exploded on their own. I would end up embarrassed, unsatisfied, and confused. I saw this as all the more reason to avoid feelings and sharing them. Can you relate to this?

There Are More Than Four Feelings

What a shock it was for me to realize how disconnected I was from my full range of feelings. I was most familiar with feeling happy, sad, angry, and confused. Those adjectives covered my bases in conversation when asked how I was feeling. I have recently begun to study Marshall Rosenberg's work as explained in his book, *Nonviolent Communication*. He extends an invitation to be more specific about expressing what a feeling is called. So, for example, when I say I feel angry, I could also say I am livid, resentful, outraged, furious, or indignant, to name a few options. Why does it matter if I use the word angry to describe that feeling all the time and not use other variations? It matters to the listener and it is also important to the speaker to be specific in identifying exactly what the feeling is because, the better and more specific the communication, the more likely it is that everyone will understand what is being related, and then needs can be met and values honored. I encourage you to summon the courage and take the time to practice this part of your self-care.

Small Action Steps

1. Start paying attention to what you are feeling at different times. Just make a mental note that you have a feeling.

2. When you notice a feeling, see if there is a corresponding physical signal, such as a headache, an upset stomach, tightness in your chest, shallow breathing, or backache.

3. What is a fear that you have about allowing yourself to experience your feelings?

4. Describe what it would be like to be confident enough to navigate your feelings safely.

Truth Telling

Some of us grew up hearing the adage, "If you don't have something nice to say about somebody, don't say anything at all." As a grumpy child and adolescent, I didn't say a whole lot as a result. I became an exceptional listener; I also shut down and didn't share anything about myself.

Do you know how to say what you really believe, what is really true for you at any given time? How does this relate to self-care? Being able to express your beliefs and ideas is the basis of authentic communication. Many of us are fearful of telling what we really think and believe. There are those of us who do speak our truths (what you value, what your perception is), and brava for them! I aspire to be like them.

I am certain you have witnessed women who are confident telling their truth and if you are like me, I experience some fear that they will be ridiculed, and almost simultaneously, I am thoroughly energized and encouraged to follow their example in my small baby steps, knowing that eventually, I'll be as comfortable as they are.

A great place to start is to be truthful with yourself. Try to be as honest as you can be about what you really want, about what responsibilities really belong to you and which ones don't, about whether what you see as a problem is really a problem, about how well you are taking care of yourself, about what role you play in a situation.

Toss Out Old Stories

We each have old stories that we drag around to justify whatever sympathy or attention we are looking for. There is a story and then there is a story. The first few times we recreate a trauma, injustice, or disappointment in order to communicate the event, we have the opportunity to publicly announce our hurt and unfulfilled feelings. We receive support for our painful condition. Many times there is therapeutic value in retelling a story for a time.

When we are using our story for shock value or as a way to remain numb to our feelings, then it's time to let the story go and get down to the business of healing and moving on. My first repeated story was about my mother's untimely demise from the mysterious disease, cancer, which wasn't well understood at the time. Over time, I was able to change my presentation of this story from a "poor me" angle to letting people know that the gift I got from losing my mother at a young age was that I really understood that there are no guarantees in life, and that being present and living each moment to the fullest makes sense. I am eternally grateful for the insight I reached which has given me fulfillment, peace of mind, courage, adventure, and growth. It has guided me since that young age, and I am pleased to be open to living life today.

My two divorces were the next stories that took the stage. I used them to make sure those I told knew that I had been "victimized." I got tired of telling the stories as time went on. That was because I did some truth telling with myself and knew that I had a part to play in those scenarios. From that truth telling, I could see that I gained much from those relationships that I am grateful for. I learned where I needed to do some personal development, and I have moved on to being in my third marriage. This partnership is showcasing the ways in which I am able now to communicate more fully and willingly and make choices based on my wants, needs, and values. I continue to move forward being more authentic, grounded, and inspired, and that brings me great joy.

Say What You Really Mean

Are you communicating from your heart, from your juicy self? Sometimes we can slip into a pattern of saying what is expected of us, and what we say may not be what we really think or feel. You will know the difference when you pay attention to what you are communicating and whether or not it rings true to your beliefs and values. If you see that you are not saying what you really think and feel, notice first of all to whom you are trying to please by speaking as you do. Listen closely to what it is that you would say if it were the genuine You speaking. Figure out what the costs are of not saying what you mean. Make a decision to change your approach and speak from your authentic self, the self you know you really are.

You may need professional help to learn how to communicate fully. There are a number of books that address this topic that could be useful as well.

State a Preference

If you are asked what you would prefer, do you make a choice? Do you ask what the other party would prefer and defer to that choice as a rule? If you find that you defer to someone else's preference fairly regularly, here is a suggestion. First of all, before you automatically respond with, "What do you think?" or "What would you like to do?", take a breath. That breath will give you pause, a chance either to give an answer if you have one or say, "Let me think about that a minute." It's okay to take time to answer. It's okay to let there be silence while you think.

This is not an easy transition to make. Sometimes deferring to someone else's decision comes from not wanting the responsibility of having made the decision in case something goes wrong. When asked which restaurant you would like to go to, what you would like to do next, when you'd like to buy the next car, take a breath. Find the courage to make a choice when one is presented.

Little by little, with practice, you will see how satisfying it is to state a preference and be a part of the decision-making process from a place of having made your desires known. There is always compromise; it is still important to have contributed what you have to offer, whether your choice is the one used or not.

Start Telling Your Truth

Telling the truth to yourself and the people around you diminishes stress and complications. Start the journey. You can begin with yourself. Listen to what you say to yourself and others about who you are and why you do what you do. See if you are relying on excuses, blaming, or ignorance. This is a process that takes time. Be patient with yourself.

Small Action Steps

1. Listen for what your old stories are. What is the old story you are ready to let go of?

2. Observe women who speak their truth. What surprises you about what they do?

3. Practice giving your preference when given a choice.

4. Name one fear you have about saying what you want.

People Pleasing

Let's define a people pleaser as someone who is compliant, who avoids conflict, and who does lots of good deeds for others. This sounds like someone who is very easy to be around, doesn't make waves, always volunteers when something needs to be done, and who doesn't complain.

It took me a very long time to understand that I have been a people pleaser for most of my life. I would hear the term "people pleaser," think it was a catchy phrase, and never imagine that it applied to me. I see myself as self-confident and independent, and so I thought there couldn't be any room for me to be a people pleaser. Yes, I liked to help people, to offer my ears, talents, and brawn (doing good deeds to boost self-worth). I could always ignore or walk away from someone saying something I didn't agree with (avoiding conflict). I would not openly discuss what I felt was out of line with my own beliefs and values (being compliant). Do you fit any of these descriptions?

How did I figure out and admit that this was a big part of how I operated? It happened on my last birthday. I was asking my husband and an out-of-town friend what they wanted to do for the rest of the day. Then they asked me what I wanted to do and decided that it would be up to me to plan the rest of the day. This was a welcome challenge. At the same time I felt enormous pressure because I was in unfamiliar territory.

It was exhausting to think about what I wanted. By the end of the day I was pleading for help deciding where to have dinner. What became crystal clear to me was how frequently I was inadvertently checking in to see what other people wanted, and that my wishes, wants, needs, and desires were covered up, hard to recognize, and unfulfilled! This was an area where I needed practice to strengthen my self-care. Some of the skills I lacked were communication techniques, awareness of my emotional triggers and how to manage them, and a healthy respect for discord and its potential gifts.

The request for me to be the decision maker and design a day based on what I wanted was a gift and a challenge. I saw how accommodating I am to other people's wishes. Very easygoing—that's me. I am so "easygoing" that I don't know what I really want or how to ask for it. My stepchildren are some of my greatest teachers. They know what they want, and I have learned negotiating skills, flexibility, and being bold in making requests by observing them. Thank you, Randi, Jay, and Betsy!

Get Friendly with Conflict

Can you imagine learning how to negotiate conflict in a constructive, beneficial exchange of ideas and beliefs? How many times have you found yourself in the midst of conflict and unable to even address the conflict? Do you remember feeling helpless even imagining that you could engage in negotiation by expressing your feelings and needs to move toward resolution? Life is change, conflict, and compromise. One of the gifts that comes from following the path of resolving conflict is learning to honor ourselves by giving and receiving empathy and compassion. We learn what our needs are, what other's needs are, and how we can work together to meet all the needs of each particular situation.

Get Back to Basics

There are some basic building blocks necessary to create the foundation for negotiating conflict. Practice speaking your mind. Find a partner, group, or therapist to help you with scenarios as you discover the way you can explain your needs. Find out what your needs are. Discover how to express what you feel and before that, practice saying what you feel through self talk, journaling, or asking a friend to help. You will learn to speak your mind in a way that can be understood and appreciated, and that will go a long way toward becoming more comfortable with the inevitable conflict that teaches us so much.

Act From the Heart, Not Out of Duty

Would you be willing to accept that your worth does not depend on how many good deeds you do for others at your own expense and personal development? Giving from the heart is an enormous gift to the giver. Giving because of a sense of duty, obligation, or way to a beautiful afterlife is less of a gift to the giver.

It is easy to measure the different feel of doing something for someone out of a sense of duty or doing something for someone out of love. Doing something for someone out of a sense of duty originates in the brain and is calculated. You will hear in your head or say out loud, "I should…". The feeling is anonymous, dry, sometimes angry, unsettling. Doing something for someone out of love originates from the center of your being, from your core, from your heart. You will hear in your head or say out loud, "I would like to do this for you…". The feeling is warm, openhearted, friendly, loving, joyous, and tender. Connecting to your heart energy is enriching, because the result is a deep relationship with what you most value. Learn to know the difference.

Say "No" Without Guilt

You can say "No" and not feel guilty or feel the need to offer an extensive explanation around your answer. Here are some reasons to say "No". You will empower yourself to take care of your own needs like ease, choice, dignity, space, and freedom. You will be practicing honesty and authenticity which is likely to bring a feeling of satisfaction and fulfillment. Saying "No" may be difficult at first. Remember that you will be creating a new behavior pattern for yourself when you begin to stop an automatic "Yes" to everything you are asked to do or be. All change involves commitment, practice and willingness to feel awkward and make mistakes as you learn.

A story that illustrated this and gave me permission to practice saying "No" is about a school staff member who telephoned a mom to ask her to make cupcakes for a school event the following day. People pleasers will consistently and "happily" take care of requests. The mom in this instance decided to say "No." The world did not fall apart, and the person who had asked the favor, went on to the next name on her list, and found someone to do the task.

Advantages of Being a People Pleaser

You rarely get involved in conflict and rarely argue. You get lots of positive response. You feel loved and needed.

Disadvantages of Being a People Pleaser

You miss out on being a receiver. You don't know your own likes and dislikes. You feel invisible. You miss out on practicing the arts of negotiation, compromise, and flexibility. You don't know when or how to say "No."

Acknowledge How Saying "Yes" or "No" Impacts Your Life

I'm not saying that "No" is the obvious and only reply. There is a difference between always saying "Yes" and making a decision about whether to say "Yes" or "No."Another way to look at this is to think about what you are saying "No" to by saying "Yes." Take the example of the cupcakes. By saying "Yes" to the cupcakes, there may have been less time for attending a child's soccer game, reading a bedtime story, or relax time with a spouse after a hectic day. Knowing that you have the option of saying "No" is very freeing, healthy, and nurturing. Another tip is to try out the phrase "In this moment, I choose me" and see how it feels when you weigh up your options to any situation.

Slow down!

Most women are multitasking athletes. Balance your multitasking with some rest periods. There's an adrenaline rush that comes with keeping your head above water within the vortex of activity and responsibility that you have accepted. Minimize the adrenaline level by scaling back. Your health may depend on it.

Small Action Steps

1. Observe how often you do things out of a sense of duty. What are some examples from the past week?

_____

_____

_____

_____

2. Let someone else volunteer.

3. Let people give to you. Notice how it feels to be a receiver.

4. Observe how often you ask, "What would you like to do?"

5. Before doing a good deed, check in with yourself to make sure you are doing it because you really want to.

Physical
Self-Care

Develop a de-cluttering **routine**

Enjoy **living in your home**

Feel comfortable **in your body**

Be confident **about**
your financial health

Get used to playing, laughing,
and having fun **more often**

Living Spaces

How do you feel in a room that is crowded, poorly lit, and stuffy? Think of the times you have felt like you wanted to exit pronto from a room or house. Then think of the times you have been in spaces where you felt relaxed or invigorated. Most of us have heard of Feng Shui, the Chinese art of placement. In extreme cases it can mean that you may have to relocate to a new residence! The lesson in this art form is connecting to the energetic relationship between yourself and your physical surroundings.

We design our living spaces. Do you agree? We have choices to make whether we own, rent, or borrow the space we live, work, and play in. Do you take responsibility for creating your spaces? Do you choose colors that you like for decorating your walls? Have you hung artwork, displayed photos, selected curtains that please you? If you don't know what your taste is, treat this as an adventure. Start noticing what is available. Window shop or look at catalogs to get an idea of what you like. Then find the courage to give yourself permission to experiment.

Address Stuff and Clutter

Do you regularly de-clutter your living spaces? We gather, accumulate, and then rent storage units to house our expanding bounty. This is a weighty proposition both energetically and physically. I speak from experience. I moved frequently at one time in my life, and during the final move of that period, I collapsed in despair on a bench outside of my beautiful new apartment. I really believed that I had pared down my belongings prior to the move, only to discover that boxes covered the entire surface area of my new living quarters, and I didn't even have room to lie down on the floor to stretch out my aching back. I had boxes and boxes of books. I had boxes and boxes of stuff. I vowed that I would not repeat the experience of lugging stuff with me that did not hold very high value and that was not truly useful.

> It is easy to forget that we are more than the possessions we acquire.

The very first time that I became aware of stuff was when my parents asked me to come and toss out or take away my childhood belongings from their attic. It was a shock to think that I would have to take a look at this stuff and decide whether I would keep it and take it with me, or let it go. I was attached to this stuff because it defined who I had been so far; it was my (her)story. And an unspoken tradition held that I would be showing these things to my grandchildren.

It is inevitable that you will accumulate possessions. We are bombarded with many affordable opportunities to purchase and bring home quantities of stuff. Most of us are blessed with more than enough.

Make an assessment to see if the balance of enjoying the stuff you have accumulated is serving your well-being or if there is a sense of desperation, depression, or numbness as a result of too much meaningless stuff surrounding you. What do you hold on to, collect, don't even remember you have? I would like to invite you to take a look around you. Start throwing out or giving away unwanted baggage.

Explore Your Stuff

I have a friend who loved the seashore. Every year she would go on vacation to the ocean and bring back bags full of seashells. Soon she was buying steamer trunks to store the shells. The happy ending to this story is that she decided to move to the Outer Banks in North Carolina and live on the beach. She satisfied her need for being near the coastline with the decision to live near the ocean, and she could live the life she was craving. P.S. She did bring her hand-picked shells in the steamer trunks with her to remind her of her passion for being a beach girl.

Take some time to consider why you feel the need to accumulate stuff. Perhaps you are clinging to the past. Perhaps you lack trust that there will always be enough of what you will need in the future. Perhaps there is an emptiness that you are trying to fill. Find the courage to explore what keeps you attached to stuff.

De-clutter, Detach, Shake It Up

Every year, usually in the spring or autumn, I do a total sweep through the house—top to bottom—and attempt to let go of what no longer fits in my wardrobe, weed out kitchen gadgets that haven't been used in years, set aside books and magazines that I am done with, and collect whatever hasn't been called into service in three years. I consider this ritual a very invigorating, courageous, and important part of my self-care. I have experienced the results of sifting and sorting and making choices in how I design my living spaces. I find tremendous freedom in keeping clutter to a minimum. We are always evolving. Being surrounded by things that have lost their meaning and value is counterproductive to growth and creativity.

Sock drawers, closets, the "miscellaneous" kitchen drawers, medicine chests, car glove compartments—the territory is endless and a vast frontier of possibility for discovery, reorganization, lightening up, clearing out, remembering, refining, refreshing, and redefining. The biggest hurdle is being overwhelmed at the prospect of de-cluttering. This is an ongoing process and it is possible to do in small, bite-sized segments. One minute is a long time. Experiment setting a timer for one to five minutes, choose one drawer to sort through and see what the result is. I believe you will be pleasantly surprised to see what you have accomplished in that short span of time. Think of the possibilities open to you when you take short time slots to keep your physical environments "alive".

Are you feeling free, light, and easy?

If you share living space with others, start with your own belongings first. Be an example and share conversation about your experience with de-cluttering. There's no need to expend energy worrying about what the rest of your household will or won't do. As a pioneer, find the strength to begin the process with confidence that you are taking great care of your own living space. The reward from that will be enough. The shifts in your energy and life circumstances will likely provide encouragement for those you share space with to become proactive in creating an environment for themselves that invites positive, welcoming, openness to new possibilities.

Do your surroundings reflect who you want to be? Are there any shifts or changes in your surroundings that will encourage and express your creative signature?

Create Sacred Space

Arrange to have sacred space somewhere in your home. By this I mean have a place where you can sit that is comfortable for you, that is decorated according to your taste, and that remains undisturbed by fellow inhabitants. This may sound like an impossible task; try it out anyway.

Sacred space is for you alone. It can be a part of the garden, a corner of a room, a shelf area, or a whole room. When you want to invite stillness, contemplation, peace, inspiration, hope, and rest, there is nothing more delicious than having a ready-made sitting place or visual creation that accommodates that need.

For me, I have a porch swing that I use regularly to soothe myself, reset my engine, and commune with nature. I also have a dresser filled with family photos of happy gatherings over the years that nurtures me. My garden is a favorite respite and in my yard there is a large boulder with a Buddha and bell that provides a seat where I can gaze at the garden and smell the air. One friend has created an entire meditation room in his home complete with antique Chinese wooden beds lavishly decorated with satin embroidered pillows and enormous statues of Indian deities and a one-foot diameter metal singing bowl. At the other end of the spectrum, if you lived in a very small space with someone else, you could hang a curtain in a corner of the room and count that as a sacred space. Be creative. Carve out a spot that will be there at all times.

> Making choices about what we want to keep in view, in boxes, and in storage units is a responsibility. Decide what is important to you. Consider the option of weeding out what no longer holds value or meaning.

Value Your Gifts

Dealing with gifts is a continual process. You will be gifted by well-meaning and loving family and friends. It is your choice and responsibility to decide if the gift is something that you wish to keep. Develop your ability to be choosy about what you will include in your physical surroundings. Some of us find it awkward and painful to even silently consider this kind of choice, while others of us are not shy or uneasy about declaring aloud what we think or feel upon opening a gift. For the awkward and pained among us, I suggest giving a questionably-welcomed gift a testing time. See if it grows on you.

I was gifted something recently that I was sure I did not want, but it has since found its place and I am very happy with it. I had received a wedding gift that was a huge painting of the seashore in the 1920s. My first reaction was one of indifference. I have little association with the ocean. I am more familiar with lakes and rivers. And I didn't know who had given the gift. The painting stayed on the floor for a few weeks, as I was using the testing time method. Eventually I discovered the identity of the giver, a friend who has a heart of gold and who is gentle and sincere. I fell in love with the painting and have discovered the perfect place to display it.

If the gift does not find its place in your heart, silently acknowledge the giver's intention of love and generosity, then let the gift go to a more suitable home.

Make Your Office Work for You

Whether you work at home, in a cubicle, in a large corporate office with a window view, or from your car, pay attention to that physical environment. Does all your equipment function well? Is it reliable? Do you have to hunt to find a file, folder, your glasses, or a piece of mail? Design an inviting physical space so that your creativity, best self, and expertise are easy to access.

Customize your office space to suit you. You are worth the time and effort. Open the door to a work space you like. If fresh flowers in your office bring you inspiration and smiles, invest in them. If having reading glasses within easy reach wherever you are will enhance your office, buy a dozen pairs of reading glasses and keep them on shelves and in drawers. In one home I visited, I noticed that there were reading glasses in the bathrooms and on the window ledge above the kitchen sink…luxury!

Drive In Style

Here's the final frontier: your car. Is your car working for you? Literally, does your car get regular maintenance? Do you feel comfortable that you are more than likely to get from A to B safely? What peace of mind to have a reliable vehicle!

Next, do you feel that you want to apologize for the interior of your car? This may be a clue that you could benefit from clearing the debris out more often! You may share your vehicle with children or other family members. Do your best. Perhaps making a request from family members to appreciate your need for order and cooperation will be useful and nurturing for you.

Small Action Steps

1. List or visually note each space that is cluttered in your home.

2. Make an appointment with yourself to devote anywhere from 15 minutes to an entire day to clearing out. Ask a friend who is efficient, fun, and willing to help you get started. Who might you consider asking for help?

3. Have a conversation with the rest of your family to discuss what clearing out will mean for you. How do you think you will feel when you clear out the clutter?

4. Start small.

5. Hire an organizer if you need help.

6. Donate your stuff.

7. Host a party or family gathering and de-clutter as you prepare for it.

8. If you find yourself commenting or thinking to yourself, "I really want to take care of that drawer, closet, room, or file cabinet" at least 3 times, commit to beginning the project the next day in 5 to 10 minute spurts. Which drawer, closet, room, or filing cabinet needs your attention right now?

Food, Exercise & Wellness

Food, exercise, and wellness are loaded topics for many women. The formula for balancing nutritious food volume with expending energy and burning calories to equal physical wellness just makes sense. And yet there is so much wrapped up in the formula that keeps many of us out of balance. Getting the checkups, massages, facials/pedicures, and time-outs that you need are sometimes left on the back burner.

Eat with Fierce Choice and Commitment

You are in charge of how you feed yourself. Do you function best by eating frequent, small meals? Are you someone who would prefer not to eat after 5 p.m.? Does breakfast at 7 a.m./8 a.m./9 a.m./10 a.m./11 a.m. give you the most benefit? One of my friends has let her household know that she does not do lunch, and that means that her husband and children are on their own for making lunch. For her, eating two meals a day works best. Decide on what you know works best for you. If you don't know, experiment to find a conclusion. Then take care of yourself by setting the boundaries you need around your eating habits.

Here are two phrases to add to your tool kit. One is "Yes, but no," in answer to the offer of food or more helpings of food. The other is "Not now, thanks." I use these very successfully in my own life.

Say "Yes, but No"

Saying "Yes, but no" when asked to accept an offer of food or drink, sends a clear message that you do want whatever it is that is being offered and are making a decision not to accept it. I have seldom had anyone try to convince me that I should change my mind. Also, I get to hear myself make two choices. One is that, yes, I sure do want another helping of eggnog, chocolate pudding, or quiche, so I am being honest with what my reality is. The other choice I hear myself making is that I will pass on the offer. This is a fulfilling method of navigating extra helpings for me. Try it out for yourself.

Say "Not Now, Thanks"

When someone offers me the option of another helping, I say "Not now, thank you." The magic of this small phrase is that the person offering the food/drink hears that you are clear that this is not the time you choose to have more. When I have said "No, thanks," I have found that the person offering the food or drink is likely to continue a conversation trying to persuade me to change my mind. For some reason, "Not now, thanks" leaves hope for the future, and the persuasion dissipates. The other thing that dissipates is the urge to have more when in fact you may have had a sufficient amount. Many of us know that our brain takes

If you've fallen, slipped, or stumbled, get up!

We all know what it's like to interrupt a routine that works for us. Just begin again, and most importantly, keep regret or criticism of yourself to a bare minimum. Forgive yourself for not being perfect. Celebrate being perfectly imperfect! Give yourself credit for the courage to start over. Whatever your reason was for stopping what was working for you is gone and unimportant. Concentrate on rediscovering your momentum, and love every small step you take. Those small steps add up to your success in moving toward what you want.

5 to 10 minutes to catch up with what our stomachs are telling us.

Get Moving to Your Own Beat

Nurturing yourself by getting the exercise you need is very important. General exercise takes care of stress levels, cardio keeps your heart healthy, and weight-bearing routines encourage healthy bones and healthy muscles. Core muscles (like abdominals) that are in good shape help you sit comfortably and stand tall. Perhaps the exercise experience can also be a bonding time with your spouse, children, friends, work colleagues, or pets.

I believe that the biggest factor affecting self-care in the exercise realm is to find what you enjoy and/or try out something new when the opportunity presents itself. I once visited a family member in the Midwest, and we went to a shopping mall. There was a trampoline set up. My first reaction was to get really excited at the prospect of using the equipment because I had loved the times I'd used a trampoline in gym classes at school. Then fear stepped in and I was willing to pass up the opportunity. Fortunately I plucked up my courage. We wore safety belts attached to bungee cords and proceeded to jump higher than high with the help of the cords. It was a blast. It was scary. It was an amazing bonding experience for my husband, step daughter, and me. I would have really regretted passing up that opportunity, and though I was initially reluctant, I knew in my heart that I had to try it out.

Answer the call of your sense of adventure. You could try a combo of activities like hiking, biking, and swimming. You may like to find a triathlon, which would keep you motivated if you like to have a goal. You may enjoy tennis games, golf, or racquetball. I love the idea of the climbing walls that are more and more accessible.

Make Sure It's Practical

The second biggest factor to making exercise a regular event in your life is to make sure it fits your lifestyle, pocketbook, and timetable. Figure out how to make the activities you choose easy enough to plan and do regularly without a lot of hassle.

Get Back on the Wagon

And the third biggest factor for success in this arena is to realize that if you have fallen off the cart, it's never too late to start again! Do not despair or give up if you have let go of your exercise commitment. This is something that happens to most of us. Just get back to it and do it. Gather support from an exercise buddy if that is what works for you. If you have never had an exercise regimen, start now. Your body will thank you most especially as you start the aging process. Your body is built to move. It wants to stay active. Gift yourself with a strong spine and flexible joints.

Modify, Modify, Modify

Always be mindful that what you were able to do for exercise, range of motion, and strength is likely to have altered as you age. Find the courage to modify an exercise so that it suits your present situation.

Trust Me, It Works

I had a three-year lapse in regular exercise, and I got back on track after going for a hike and a bike ride on two separate occasions and seeing how out of shape I was. I spent a few days remembering what works best for me to stay on a routine. For me, exercise needs to happen first thing in the morning or it doesn't happen at all. I also need to be outside if at all possible, and I am most motivated if I don't have to get into my car to go somewhere to exercise. These are truths about how I tick. I have also overcome a resistance or two and taken the steps to follow through.

Is my exercise routine ideal and "perfect"? No, and that's okay. I am feeling very successful in having crafted a routine that gives me the basics that keep me getting up each morning, putting on my sneakers, and going out the door to walk. I have set a goal of fast walking, measured the course, and I occasionally check in with my progress. I feel relieved to be exercising again.

A Salute to Abdominal Muscles

One time in my teenage years I was standing next to a car that had stopped in my neighborhood, and one of the girls from my school was sitting in the backseat. She was not leaning against the back of the seat. I"m pretty sure that my mouth dropped open in amazement and disbelief that this was a possibility. I knew for myself that my back hurt even when using the support of a chair back.

I didn't know where my abs were until I was in my late forties. I had attended aerobic classes for years, done yoga, taken cycling classes and dance classes. Instructors would say, "Tighten your abs!" I kept trying to locate them—to no avail. I sincerely wanted to know how to access them because as core muscles, they are really important! Finally, finally when learning Pilates on the Reformer machine, I found what I had been looking for! The result of strengthening my abdominal muscles is that my lower back doesn't ache anymore, and I am able to sit up straight without leaning against the back of a chair for long periods of time. I am grateful to be able to sit upright on my own. I encourage you to do what you can to gain the support of your core muscles to give you ease of movement and to stand and sit in comfort.

Plan For and Practice Peak Health

Your overall physical well-being has a large impact on how you are in the world. If you have poor health, chronic pain, and/or low energy, life can feel lackluster and like hard work. Do you get regular checkups with your doctor, dentist, and dermatologist? Are you always last on the list to schedule time to take care of yourself? Remember the oxygen mask preflight instructions, which suggest that before you can effectively offer help to those around you, you must take care of getting your air supply in order. If the reason for lack of attention is finances, take steps to begin budgeting or finding clinics where you will get the care you need.

There is lasting value in learning what well-being feels like. For example, massage can teach relaxation techniques that can be used in a variety of ways. One of my massage clients told me that she survived her labor pains by imagining she was on the massage table relaxing. When I receive a facial I know that I will be totally relaxed by the end, and I relish feeling that way for an hour a month.

Take Yourself Away

The services that we sometimes view as nonessential may actually be vital to our well-being. Not everyone enjoys the same kinds of attentions to their body. I am not crazy about pedicures or manicures, and I am dedicated to getting regular facials and massages. Experiment with what "takes you away". One of my ultimate "takes me away" experiences was a mud pool with a natural waterfall nearby. My skin felt like a newborn baby's after the soak and rinse. When I was under the waterfall I stretched out my hand thinking I could turn down the water pressure! One of my simplest and easiest "takes me away" experiences is giving myself a foot massage.

Small Action Steps

1. Take a look at what's in your kitchen cupboards. Do you need help to create a healthier selection of ingredients and recipes?

2. Take cooking classes with your spouse, children or friend.

3. Watch the cooking channel on TV.

4. Make appointments for a physical and to see the dentist or dermatologist if it has been too long since the last ones. What appointments do you need to schedule before the end of the year?

5. Team up with friends or neighbors to do a 5K walk. Who would you invite to join you?

Money

Money is a large part of many of our lives that takes up lots of time and energy. We think about how much money we don't have, how much money we wish we had, how much money we do have, how much money our neighbors have, how much money our favorite stars have, how much money our bosses have. We may wonder what it is really like to have a billion dollars in a bank account. How much time do you spend on money issues, problems, and plans?

I know that I feel much more comfortable and secure when I have more than enough money to pay my bills and to take vacations throughout the year without feeling a tight pinch in my bank account. Perhaps you would like to accept a challenge to yourself to create a solid financial foundation and credit line so that you increase your feeling of ease and prosperity.

Take Good Care of Yourself and Your Money

Self-care in your financial realm might require you to first of all get the whole truth about your current situation. Most of us did not have formal training in money management, and we learn as we go. What can you do to get started?

If you share your finances with a spouse or partner, the best scenario is to do this together, if possible. Either way, come to grips with what you owe and what your income is after taxes. This is a huge step. If you have an issue with avoidance, then the idea of seeing the facts on paper can feel overwhelming. The good news is that knowing where you are for sure gives you a place to work from. Guessing about your financial status will keep you in limbo and, most likely, uncomfortable deep down, even though it may seem easier to remain confused or in denial.

Rally your courage and take a close look at where you stand. Face your debt, spending habits, and saving habits. Become intimate with what makes you tick in your financial environment. This is self-care that will support you as you take steps to build a stronger foundation. There is an opportunity for greater confidence in yourself if you know that you have a working picture of your finances and what you need to do to be independent and solvent. I have heard plenty of success stories from people who have turned around their heavy debt and lack of savings.

Examine Your Beliefs About Money

Do you know what your beliefs are about money? What are the beliefs that your parents, grandparents, culture, religion, and society hold about money? There are many hidden beliefs regarding money rattling around in our subconscious space. We have adopted, learned, and fabricated ideas about where money comes from and why it does or doesn't land in our wallets and bank accounts! How does money impact your life? Uncover you own beliefs about how you want to view and use money. The journey to discover your relationship with money is well worth your time and effort. Examine your present philosophies around money. See if they are true for you today. If they are not, make the necessary adjustments.

Find a financial advisor or money coach you trust to help you. Ask friends and colleagues to give you recommendations for experienced professionals they have used or know about. Get educated about how money can best support you. Why is this important? Because unless you have a special interest in investments and the Wall Street Journal, you will benefit from getting expert help and guidance. Get the help you need to have a financial base that will nurture you. Once again, this may take longer than you think. Don't let the time factor stop you in your tracks. If you don't even get started, then you're nowhere nearer your solution. If you do get started, each small step you take gets you to where you are going.

Find Your Focus

I have heard more than once that the Law of Attraction (what you think about most consistently is what you will attract) can be useful. One place to start is to get clear about what your present financial situation is, in dollars and cents. You will make a plan from there. If your plan is to eliminate debt, you may want to move your focus from concentrating on your debt. Have the steps in place to address that problem, and then choose to envision what you are moving toward. What can happen by focusing entirely on debt is that you will attract even more debt. Try paying more attention to what is coming in financially. Set your attention on incoming money.

One important factor to consider is that you have a working plan for minimizing your debt, which could be in the form of a budget or getting a part-time job to supplement what you are already earning. Once you have the plan and apply it, focus on watching the money that comes into your life. Also, be clear about what financial abundance will bring you. Is it security, more free time, contribution to something for a legacy?

Read About It

Educate yourself about money. There are plenty of resources in the library, on the Internet, and in the community. I mentioned earlier that most of us do not have formal training in money management. Understanding how credit cards work is vitally important. How much of the fine print do you read in your financial dealings? If you don't want to read all the fine print, ask around until you find someone who will educate you. What you don't know can bring a heap of suffering when, for example, you face credit card interest rates. Teach yourself and teach your children how to balance checking accounts, manage credit cards, debit cards, and ATM cards. Be a savvy consumer when you sign up for and use easy-to-access money.

Small Action Steps

1. Ask yourself if you are courageous and ready to get the true picture of your financial situation.

2. Start to collect loose change in a jar. Where will you keep the jar?

3. Write down 3 beliefs you have about money and where they came from.

4. Ask colleagues, friends, and family to recommend a financial advisor.

5. Check out www.cheapskatemonthly.com to find Mary Hunt's helpful hints to debt-proof living.

Play & Laughter

I'd like to ask you to take a few minutes to remember the last time you were playful; playing without competition, with full abandon, with the joy of possibility and discovery. Was it today, yesterday, last week, last month, last year? Let's hope you didn't answer last year!

Lighten Up

It can be easy to forget to not take things so seriously. It can be easy to forget that it is okay to interrupt your schedule to take a minute or more to splash in a puddle, look goofy, appreciate a silly moment, or make up and sing a silly song. Give yourself great self-care by remembering to play frequently…even if you don't feel like it to begin with…even if it means having to teach yourself to let go and be playful and silly.

Do the Juggling Dance

I recently attended a dance class. One of the guided exercises was to pretend we were juggling while moving around the floor to music. I found myself captivated by the activity and could feel the layers of "formal adult" start to drop away as I focused on pretending to juggle based on what I remembered from watching people who could! I came face to face with another woman who started tossing me her pretend juggling objects, and I started to feel the excitement of being five years old and playing a game that someone had invited me to join. The feeling in my chest was sheer joy and excitement.

Many times we get wound up with responsibilities that we accept, wound up with codes of behavior, and we forget to unwind to keep our balance. Be open and willing to play and when you are able, initiate the game. Your energetic self will feel sparkly and light.

Hula Hoop

I resurrected my dusty hula hoop from the basement and brought it upstairs. Friends were visiting one evening and using our collective imaginations and energies, we had some play time with the hula hoop that felt light, fun, refreshing, and inclusive. It took me a while before I tried the hula-hoop-around-the-neck-trick. I knew I used to do it as a kid. One of my friends did it effortlessly. I was fully aware of the fears I had as I watched thinking, "Oh my God, she's going to hurt her neck!" I worked up the courage to try it later and, sure enough, I could do it easily.

We learn from experience about caution and sometimes we limit ourselves too much from letting go and seeing if something is possible. Sometimes we learn to believe that we're too old to play, that we'll hurt ourselves, that we have an image that we are too responsible to take time to play, that we can't afford the time to play, that we'll look foolish if we skip around the room spontaneously! It's okay to work at being playful. We forget the value of playtime as we get older. As with everything, remember to modify the ways in which you choose to play according to your ability and flexibility!

Giggle

I define giggles as the short form of a belly laugh. They are just as effective! If you have misplaced the giggle inside of you, find it. Give yourself the space and freedom to lighten up. Spend time with people who encourage you to giggle, people who giggle easily themselves. I was leading a meditation group once, and one of the participants started to giggle. She left the room because she was not able to stop whatever had tickled her funny bone. I enjoyed her giggling as much as she did because I know from my own experience how good it feels to be caught up in the uncontrollable lightness of being, whenever and wherever I am. Plus, it was a subtle reminder to me to be open to the giggles in my own experience!

> The flip side is a good cry! Both experiences are healthy ways to release our energies. Let yourself be open.

Laugh

There are many types of laughter, and they run the gamut from mirth to derision. The key to recognizing laughter that empowers self-care is to invite the kind of laughter that leaves us with a triumphant sense of well-being, a feeling of joyful exuberance. A good belly laugh is priceless for me. Let's not forget the delight of an exhausting belly laugh that makes your face ache from smiling and the sides of your ribs tender from convulsive giggling.

There is a form of yoga termed "laughter yoga." As I understand it, you start out pretending to laugh, and you eventually end up laughing naturally. Try this out with a friend or two.

Small Action Steps

1. Listen to funny audio tapes or watch funny movies. Which movies make you laugh? Who is your favorite comedian?

2. Watch children play to refresh your memory of silliness and imagination.

3. Get on the floor and see life from the eyes of small children or pets. What do you notice?

4. Look at the *Reader's Digest* humor section. Go to the library and look at the *The New Yorker* cartoons.

Body Language

How do hips, sex, and body posture fit together? For many of us, there have been years and years filled with shame and guilt and judgment about our bodies and our sexuality. Add to that the tendency to live in our heads and the result is a disconnect from our physicality, sensation and pleasure. We become comfortably numb. By bringing attention to the hips, body posture and sexuality, I hope that you will take a leap if any of these areas need adjustment so that you will find complete fulfillment in who you are as a being in the fantastic vehicle of the female form!

> *She is moving to describe the world... Divine, to Define... The world moves on a woman's hips...*
>
> —Talking Heads. "The Great Curve"[7]

Swing Those Hips

As a body worker, I "people watch" to observe movement and walking patterns. The mechanics of movement are wondrous and filled with variety! Take care of your body by using it as it was designed. Rotating your hips may help improve a natural walking gait. It takes pressure off the knees and ankles if you move from your pelvic area when walking. Many of us lock our bodies from the waist down. Many of us lock our knees when we walk. Observe what your walking pattern is. See if there is anything you can improve to keep comfortable as you walk. Keep walking in your daily activity. The body is meant to move, and sitting all day long is exhausting, believe it or not. So for basic, simple self-care, walk each day.

Ignore the Floozie Factor

For those of you who don't know, a floozie is defined by the dictionary as "a woman regarded as gaudy or tawdry."[8] Other people's perception of the floozie factor may be part of the problem for some of us who walk with minimal hip movement. Some of us were raised to think that flaunting our bodies was undesirable and so the less movement, the better. I love watching women who are fluid in their body movements. They are my role models. I have to consciously swing my hips, and I look forward to the day that the swinging hips will happen naturally. Take care of yourself and let your hips sway!

Realign Your Posture

This is a reminder to stand tall. I use "stand tall" instead of "stand up straight" because I am betting that many of you heard a plea from a parent to "stand up straight!" I never understood how to achieve a naturally upright posture with that command. I would throw my shoulders back military style and lock my knees. I was so uncomfortable that my face was contorted in agony. It never looked like an improvement from slouching to me!

Many years later, I get how to be in a natural upright posture. And what is the benefit of practicing standing tall? As we age we tend to "cave in" at the shoulders and "stoop down" with our heads leaning forward. I once saw a yoga instructor take four steps across the stage and show the progression of posture as we age. What a powerful vision and an inspiration to keep upright.

Let's see if you can find a difference in how it feels to "stand tall" by following these steps.

The Ribbon Exercise

Stand up. Relax your knees by bending them slightly. Imagine that there is a ribbon attached to your upper chest at a 45-degree angle, and it is pulling you toward the ceiling. This image helps to lift your rib cage. Next, imagine that there is another ribbon attached to the center of the top of your head, and it is also pulling you up to the ceiling. If your head tends to pitch forward on your neck, this image will help realign it. Relax into each part of this exercise, breathe, and repeat until you feel comfortable. Look in the mirror as you try repositioning yourself. Keep repeating until it becomes second nature to stand in this position.

Be Your Own Sexy Lady

Everyone has their own needs in their sexuality. What I'd like to encourage you to do is to review and assess for yourself what is working and what needs improvement about your sexual self. Are there questions you need to have answered? Is there open communication with your partner, and if there isn't, are you willing and prepared to have those conversations?

Alexander Technique

A method of reeducating the body and mind to overcome poor habits of posture and movement and to reduce physical and mental tension.

Feldenkrais Method

Aim is to restore the ability to move as freely and spontaneously as a child, liberated from body habits that contribute to a myriad of health problems.

Rolfing

Increases muscular length and overall balance for optimal posture.

Is it a struggle to talk about sex even with girlfriends or sisters? What is your image of your sexual self? Is it tied up with media standards? Do you appreciate yourself for exactly who you are at this minute in your body? Are you worthy of having pleasure? How well do you know your own body? Do you need to spend time with yourself exploring what works for you? Do you make time for sex? It is never too late to learn what pleases you. It is never too late to teach a willing partner how to please you.

In your assessment of your sex life, be honest with yourself about what is missing, and celebrate with yourself if everything in this area is fully satisfying! Get the help you need if there are areas that are uncomfortable for you and need improvement. Get more education or professional counseling to help move you along to a place where you can be active and satisfied. Be proactive to ensure that you have a healthy relationship with your sexuality. Most importantly, allow time for sex. It is not unusual to discover that this facet of your life has taken a backseat to everything else. Appreciating your sexuality and physical body is purely individual. Find the courage to understand what works for you.

Small Action Steps

1. If you need help with your posture, find a professional to guide you. Make an appointment with a Rolfer, a massage therapist, a yoga teacher, Alexander teacher, or Feldenkrais practitioner.

2. Honestly decide if your sex life is in need of improvement.

3. Make a date with your spouse or partner or yourself to discuss what you would like to improve in your sexual relationship.

4. How can you celebrate your sexuality this week?

5. Let go of judgment. Stand nude in front of a mirror and see your beauty.

6. Have a conversation with a friend about the advantages of being a woman.

7. Attend a belly dancing class.

Spiritual
Self-Care

Become familiar with the power **of your breath**

Spark your creativity

Know what inspires **you**

Express **your gratitude daily**

Breath

When was the last time you took a really deep breath? Many of us use only a fraction of our lung capacity. Most of us don't even think about our next breath. It is automatic, built into our body mechanism. Why bother? A client recently described in glorious detail her first sensation of a deep, relaxed breath after a lifetime of shallow, restricted breathing. She said she could taste air for the first time; that she could actually feel the air in her lungs for the first time. Her muscles—her body—relaxed for the very first time. This was a unique and life-changing event for her. She got perspective about how uneasy and tense her body had been for as long as she could remember! What a beautiful experience, to discover a way to relax!

We have the option of accessing our breath to help us de-stress at any time, and yet it is easy to forget to use it. As our lives become more fast-paced, we often get used to breathing in quick, shallow breaths or, on the opposite end, we hold our breath. Start checking in with yourself to monitor how you are breathing. This will give you a baseline for recognizing your patterns, especially in stressful situations.

Picture a Pomegranate

A favorite exercise I like to use is to imagine what's happening when we begin to practice taking a deeper breath by visualizing the sacs inside a pomegranate. Our lungs are lined with lots of alveoli, which look something like the inside of a pomegranate. All of those sac-like compartments are hungry for air. The deeper the breath we can take, the greater the number of those sacs will be used for proper oxygen/carbon dioxide exchange. The brain and body need a good oxygen supply to function well.

Practice Deeper Breathing

Try this experiment: When you are ready to go to sleep, try taking a long, slow, deep breath. Hold the air in your lungs for as long as you can, and then slowly exhale. You may be amazed at the feeling of having expanded lungs. It may even feel uncomfortable at first. Practice this for a week, trying to breathe more deeply each night. Then try taking deep breaths periodically during the day. Begin by doing this experiment while you are stopped waiting for a red light to turn green, in an elevator, before eating a meal, or any other time when you have a few seconds. Make use of your lungs!

Using your breath to break a cycle of reaction is one great tool in self-care. You are likely to reduce the stress of great agitation and your physical, emotional, spiritual, and intellectual self will thank you.

Break the Cycle

In times of turmoil, try taking a few deep breaths, or even shallow ones, to discharge pent-up energy so that it doesn't exit your body in angry words or actions that you will regret later. As a parent, teacher, or childcare worker, taking a few moments to breathe may help to de-escalate a situation with trying, crying children, friends, or spouses! One great advantage to accessing your breath is that what you say in the next breath may be less damaging, less hurtful, and more accurately in sync with what you are truly feeling.

Breath can help break the cycle of emotional turmoil. Sometimes we have patterns of behavior that seem to have lives of their own and manifest during times when we feel the need to defend ourselves. We "get on a roll" and can't seem to change it even when we realize while we're in the middle of it that it won't be productive. I have had lots of experience watching myself get taken over by my reaction to something and then using a flurry of accusations, defensiveness, and increased voice volume. I wanted to respond differently and needed practice and tips on how to do it.

Be Aware that You Forgot

Changes don't usually happen overnight, so be patient with yourself. The best you may be able to do when you first start learning to take a breath in tense situations is to remember afterward that you forgot to take a breath. Believe it or not, this is a first and important step. It is the step by which you invite the possibility of a different way. Gradually, you will have the awareness in time to take action. You will understand that stopping to take a breath is likely to be helpful.

Small Action Steps

1. When you go to bed, before you sleep, practice breathing in more deeply than you usually do. Hold the air in your lungs for a few seconds, and then breathe out more slowly than usual.

2. Before you answer someone in anger, take a few breaths.

3. Notice if you are breathing or holding your breath during the day.

4. When you are at a red light, practice breathing in and out slowly and deeply.

5. Give an example of a time when taking a breath has been useful to you during a time of stress or conflict.

Meditation & Prayer

Our lives have changed in the last 50 years with an increase in leisure time and with the luxury of modern conveniences. We can shop anytime of the day or night; we have the Internet to give us information at any time, day or night. We seem to lead abundant and privileged lives in comparison with our grandparents. So why is there so much stress and overwhelm?

Know How Fast You Are Going

I used to drive a car that told me how fast I was going without looking at the speedometer. There was no air conditioner, so when the windows were open I could hear the rush of air; the suspension was shaky, so the car shook at fast speeds. Driving my sister's new car, I found I was going ninety miles an hour but thinking I was going sixty. With its high-tech engineering, there was no road noise, no bumpy shaking. I was speeding up without realizing how fast I was going.

Time Pie-Chart

Our everyday lives are speeded up in ways we don't notice. As a result we are juggling more decisions and opportunities at a faster pace than ever before. Our minds are constantly and quickly choosing, evaluating, and seeking. Technology smooths the routine of everyday life, creating convenience and less work, but at the same time we are bombarded with input. How many radio and TV stations do you have to choose from every day? Can you keep up with the abundance of options? With more time available, how many more activities are you including each week, and are they providing a feeling of social connection? Are they worthwhile? What percentage of your time pie chart includes stillness and silence?

Would you like to try an exercise right now to see what your pie chart might look like? Get a piece of paper and a pen (or go to a beach and use a stick or your finger to write in the sand!). Write down six methods you use to slowdown and relax. Then draw a circle and divide the circle into six pie segments. Now, assign each relaxation or centering method you just wrote down to a pie segment. Then write in how many times a week or month you use that method to unwind. This is a great way to check up on yourself to make sure that you are successfully using ways to create space and calm in your life. Did you easily come up with six methods at the start of the exercise? Do you still get value from the ways you spend your time to recharge?

Find a Form of Meditation

Slowing down the pace of life today is a requirement. Meditation is a long-used method of slowing down. There are a variety of ways to meditate. You can sit, walk, or wash dishes while meditating. Wash dishes? Believe it or not, I find dish-washing after a meal a wonderful time for meditating. I am absorbed in the space of stillness between a meal and the evening's activities. Experiment with ways to include passive and active forms of meditation into your life. If you are new to meditation, talk to people with experience. There is a no need to restrict your ideas about technique by visualizing sitting in a lotus position as a necessity (especially after a certain age!).

Detach from Your Thoughts

Our exquisite brains are masterful at offering thought after thought after thought. Part of healthy self-care is to create periods of stillness from our thoughts because space from thinking is essential to life balance. It is easy to have a sleepless night because we haven't turned off the thought stream. It is easy to live in our brains and disconnect from our hearts, feelings, and inner peace when we continually think, plan, and do. It takes commitment to learn for yourself how your mind operates and to find an effective and healthy method for letting go of following every thought that passes through your brain. You will need courage to add stillness and silence in your life because being comfortable with "nothingness" will be difficult at first. This exercise needs to be practiced, and you will need the desire to practice. I believe you will enjoy the benefits immensely.

Find Your Center

Creating the time to slow down through meditation can be one of the most powerful gifts you can give yourself for nurturing you. Some rewards of meditation are feelings of being centered, at ease, and focused. The benefit of centering, ease, and focus is that you'll have a chance to get perspective. Without perspective, we can get way off track.

Say a Little Prayer

I have read some prayers that have touched me deeply. A prayer can sometimes seem to me like poetry, and there are some poems that speak to me as prayers. Be on the lookout for prayers that resonate with you. When you find a prayer or poem that strikes a chord in your heart, copy or write it down and refer to your collection when needed. This is a form of support for you in taking care of yourself. Use your creativity to appeal to your Higher Power for help or to express thankfulness. Make up your own prayers. Find prayers that speak to you.

Small Action Steps

1. Talk to friends about meditation and see if anyone you know has experience with it.

2. For one week, find 5 minutes each day to sit in silence.

3. Find or create a new prayer.

4. What happens when you give yourself silent time? What are the benefits?

_____

_____

_____

_____

_____

Creativity

I struggled for many years learning to trust that I am a creative being, that I can create my own art. Perhaps you have, too. I have discovered that one of my art forms is my life! Taking note of how you accept or are in the process of accepting that you are creative is an important way to nurture yourself because there is a simple yet exotic and unique feeling to understanding that part of yourself.

Choose to Explore and Express the Creative Part of You

Education, good grades, and academic achievement are highly valued in my family tradition. I accepted the task of doing well in school. I love learning and could be happy living in a library doing research forever more. I decided after getting my B.A., however, that I would put formal academic work on the shelf. This was a leap of faith. I knew I could easily continue the path to a Masters and Ph.D. I had fully grasped reason and logic and the mechanics of academia. Something I knew that I had little understanding of was my creative self, and I dared to dream that I could learn how to be creative.

A dictionary definition of creativity is "characterized by originality and expressiveness; imaginative."[9] I was a beginner in those three realms. I was a better copier than originator, I was best at keeping myself to myself rather than being expressive, and with the help of the educational system of the time, I had buried my imagination.

Many of us have stories to tell about how our creativity was squashed in childhood. Apart from a third grade experience with a derogatory comment from my art teacher in front of the whole class, the next time I felt inadequate in my creativity was during a summer vacation with a favorite cousin who is enormously blessed with oodles of artistic talent. My attempt at an oil painting was profoundly disappointing; even my loving cousin could only shake her head in agreement that the effort was a "failure."

There's Always More Than One Way

Fast forward to many years later, and with new confidence in my creativity, I was staring at an artistic attempt to draw something that wasn't what I had hoped for. A dear friend who was nearby asked what I was looking at and I told her of my dilemma and frustration. She asked if she could help and took a brush, worked a few lines together, and basically created a new canvas where I could continue with a different plan—and with the confidence that creativity is a process and open-ended.

Choose self-expression over self-oppression

Do an experiment and see how your body feels when you focus on self-expression. Then focus on self-oppression and observe how your body feels. Which would you like to have more of? Think about it.

Relish Young Originals

I recently attended an informal piano recital for children aged 7 to 12 years old. I was stunned and thrilled to notice that each child performed his or her own composition as part of the evening program. What freedom and encouragement to explore their own style of creativity their teacher had offered them! The children were handed the possibility and promise of their creative expression. I could see the pride and confidence in the students' faces as they played "their own songs." A far cry from the piano lessons I remember as a child!

Join an Artist's Way Group

I enrolled in a series of classes based on Julia Cameron's book, *The Artist's Way*. This book and the group of people I attended the classes with were enormously successful and supportive in helping propel me toward confidence in my creative self. If you can't find a group in your area, I highly recommend reading the book on your own.

Use Your Life as a Creative Playground

Everyone has the opportunity to add the power of creativity to their lives. Bearing and raising children is a creative venture. Here are more creative ventures: crafting a garden, learning new skills, traveling to new locations, experimenting with new foods, trying new hair styles, trying color on white walls in your home, attending concerts, joining a local performance company to try acting, creating or buying a statue or sculpture for your yard, going on a picnic with your friend, visiting a museum. The way you live your own life is a creative venture. Open your mind to the ways you can create beauty in your home, your relationships, and your work.

Make it up as you go along. Get used to forfeiting perfection and control for the joy of creating fun, joy, and meaningful moments. Experiment with art forms that have sparked an interest for you. If a venture doesn't resonate, move on to something else. I tried working with metal at one point and quickly discovered that I preferred wood or clay. It's okay to be willing to try new ways and mediums to express your creativity. Give yourself permission!

Small Action Steps

1. Get a copy of *The Artist's Way* and read it.

2. Be creative today.

3. What is one art form you would like to try?

4. Ask a friend or family member to join you in a creative endeavor: visit a museum or local art show, attend a play, or get chalk and find a sidewalk to decorate.

5. Using your imagination, create the Ideal Day for you and write it down, paint it, sing it, or dance it. Your level of skill is unimportant. Just do the best you can, and leave your judgments at the door.

Inspiration

Life can feel ho-hum and numb without inspiration. When I am inspired I can taste the joy of being alive. I have a great appreciation of the value of inspiration. Being inspired adds juice to my everyday life. What does inspiration have to do with self-care? I know that when I am feeling inspired, life is easier. Problems have less impact. In a way, I can watch life flow and "fall together" when I am operating from a place of inspiration. My attention is on the big picture. This is not about a fantasy escape. Inspiration is a tool to attract what I want to have in my life. I gain the confidence to behave as my most magnificent self! I know that I can dream big and all things are possible.

Live a Life of Inspiration, Confidence & Joy

Do you know what inspires you? It is easy to find inspiration in books, websites, posters, cards, songs, movies, plays, stories in newspapers and magazines, neighbors, strangers, Greek mythology, your faith, friends, Nature, pets. You will know what works for you when you see it or hear it. You may notice a feeling of increased energy; also, perhaps a heart connection to a larger idea or vision of yourself.

Sources of inspiration may change as you age. I couldn't live without a steady stream of music as a young adult. I am inspired now by silence and the sounds of nature. One thing I often hear from role models who inspire me is that they consider themselves to be ordinary people. This statement is powerfully encouraging because I can see that someone else has traveled a path that is open to me, too! Be kind to yourself and find inspiration to keep you buoyant and aware of possibility in your own life.

Being inspired is an experience of joy: we feel completely connected to our Source...we bring exceptionally high energy to our daily life. Our heart sings in appreciation for every breath; and we're tolerant, joyful, and loving.

—Dr. Wayne Dyer[10]

Small Action Steps

1. Find something in Nature that is inspiring…a sunset, a view, a bug, a birdsong. Let yourself feel inspired and take the time to write down what you notice.

2. Read an inspiring book, article, or poem.

3. Think of 3 ways you can add inspiration to your daily life and list them.

4. Speak with a friend or family member about inspiration and share ideas.

Gratitude & Mindfulness

We are used to being grateful for the big events in our lives, such as successful births, surgeries, new jobs, and kind weather for weddings held outdoors. But when you start to bring gratitude to the smaller events of your life, to the everyday mechanics of life, you will begin to acknowledge that you are being cared for in more ways than you think.

Starting from a place of gratitude sets the stage for self-care because we begin with what is working for us in our daily lives, and that helps us feel positive. Here are examples of everyday occurrences that you may realize you are thankful for: Waking up and moving through your day easily in a healthy body, having a conversation with a loved one and feeling deeply connected, getting to and from your job safely, having running hot and cold water in your home. Acknowledging the ways that you feel grateful each day is a habit that may manifest many benefits for you.

Enjoy the Benefits of Gratitude

When I feel that I am being cared for, I find the strength to make sure that I take care of myself. When I take care of myself physically, mentally, and spiritually, then I operate on fully charged batteries. I am hopeful, energized, and smiling. Getting familiar with recognizing ways to be grateful—developing an attitude of gratitude—builds a buffer zone, too, so that when life doesn't seem so wonderful, you will be able to find places in your life that are wonderful and nourishing.

With lots of practice you may find that you are able to be grateful for all of your experiences, even the ones that don't appear to be positive or feel good at the time. How could I be grateful for my divorce experiences? What I learned was invaluable to my growth and personal development. How could I be grateful for the death of a parent at an early age? I am thankful to have learned so quickly that there are no guarantees in life and that it is important to live each day to the fullest.

Practice Mindfulness

Mindfulness is attentiveness. It is a way of being, a way of living all the moments of your life in full awareness. Living fully in the present moment is the key. If you choose to practice mindfulness you will benefit from appreciating what is right in front of you. There is an abundance of mystery and magic in your life and when you are mindful of your surroundings, you will find ways to nurture your inner peace and joy without spending a penny. Just for this moment, focus on your breath, focus on your surroundings, focus on your sense of physical well being. Be amazed that you never even think about the mechanics of how to breathe, digest, get up from your chair. Be amazed that you live where you live and have running, drinkable water within easy reach. Be amazed that you are pain free, toothache free, healthy. I was fortunate in hindsight to have been constantly prompted to pay attention as a child. I grew up knowing how to focus, how to be present.

> *Mindfulness is a lifetime's journey along a path that ultimately leads nowhere, only to who you are. The way of awareness is always here, always accessible to you in each moment.*
>
> —Jon Kabat-Zinn[11]

It is possible to navigate stress, discomfort, confusion, and despair in a positive, creative way by practicing mindfulness. Find the rhythm of life and watch the ebb and flow, rock and roll, and peaks and valleys as they appear in your path. You will innately know that gifts and options are included in the package. Life is ready for you to open them when you are ready!

Switch Off of Automatic Pilot

> **Live your life one juicy, joyful moment at a time!**
>
> Be on the lookout for what is happening for you right here, right now. Maximize your experience of life by paying attention. Discover your hidden or forgotten desires and talents.

You have probably had the experience of asking someone when they added the new picture/rug/wall color/stove to their home décor, only to find that what you are seeing has been there for a long time.

Many of us are living on automatic pilot. Our senses are numb. How often do you really taste what you are eating? Are you smelling the flowers you pass by? Have you looked up at the night sky in the past week?

Pay Attention

One of the easiest and most convenient places to practice mindfulness is to get out and observe Nature. You can even do this in a city setting. Take a walk. Sit on a park bench. Spend time near a stream, river, lake, or ocean. Listen and watch. Pay attention to your senses. Pick up a leaf or rock or let a butterfly sit on your hand. I am never tired of watching humming birds. I am always in a state of amazement and wonder.

Try eating a meal slowly, with the intention of savoring the tastes and textures of the foods you are eating. Drink your food and eat your soup. Really listen when someone is speaking to you. Slow down so that you are entirely focused on the speaker's words. If someone gives you a compliment, receive it. Be willing to graciously accept the compliment rather than brushing it away.

Small Action Steps

1. Write a love letter to yourself and send it to yourself.

2. List 3 things you are grateful for at this moment.

3. What are you noticing about kindness that you have given or received today?

4. Try listening to someone with total attention and openness.

A Gift for You

I would like to send you off now with encouragement and plenty of cheerleading to free yourself from what keeps you hidden from view, fearful of your brilliance, and gripped with inertia regarding how to nurture and care for your self.

Here's the alphabet I've designed to help you learn the language of self-care. Have fun with it. I'd love to hear about your journey and insights as you become fluent.

Feel free to tear the page out and keep it with you to remind you that you are an amazing woman!

Alphabet for the Language of Self-Care

Adventure, Authenticity
Boundaries
Creativity, Curiosity, Courage, Clarity, Choice
Daring, Discovery
Ease
Flowing, Flexibility
Giggles, Gentleness
Health
Inspiration, Inner Peace, Integrity
Joy
Kindness
Laughter
Mindfulness, Modify, Modify, Modify
Needs, No
Openness
Play, Patience, Permission
Queenliness
Rest, Respect
Sexual Expression, Support, Small Action Steps
Truth Telling
Understood
Vulnerability
Wisdom, Willingness
X chromosome, Xtreme Self-Care
You, Yourself, Yeast-Free
Zesty, Zany

Resources

Clutter

Clear Your Clutter with Feng Shui, by Karen Kingston

It's All Too Much, by Peter Walsh

Communication

Non-Violent Communication: A Language of Life, by Marshall Rosenberg

Creativity

The Artist's Way, by Julia Cameron

Emotional

Loving What Is, by Byron Katie
The Four Agreements, by Don Miguel Ruiz
When You Eat at the Refrigerator, Pull Up a Chair, by Geneen Roth
www.avatar.com

Financial

Creating Money, by Sanaya Roman and Duane Packer
On My Own Two Feet, by Manisha Thakor and Sharon Kedar

Secrets of the Millionaire Mind, by T. Harv Eker
www.debtproofliving.com

Inspirational

Inspiration: Your Ultimate Calling, by Dr. Wayne Dyer
www.marianne.com Marianne Williamson books, audio products
www.oriahmountaindreamer.com

Sexuality/Sensuality

The S Factor: Strip Workouts for the Everyday Woman, by Sheila Kelley
www.bettydodson.com

Spirituality

The Seat of the Soul, by Gary Zukav
Power of Now, by Eckhart Tolle
Inviting Silence, by Gunilla Norris
www.spiritualcinema.com

Wellness

The Encyclopedia of Alternative Health Care, by Kristin Olsen
Full Catastrophe Living, by Jon Kabat-Zinn
Women's Bodies, Women's Wisdom: Creating Physical and Emotional Health and Healing, by Christiane Northup

Notes

1. *The American Heritage College Dictionary*, 3rd edition, page 1237.

2. Ibid., page 735.

3. *The American Heritage College Dictionary*, 3rd edition, page 169.

5. http://www.quotationpage.com, Quotation #38694.

6. *The American Heritage College Dictionary*, 3rd edition, page 282.

7. Talking Heads, *The Great Curve*, track 3 "Remain in Light," October 1980.

8. *The American Heritage College Dictionary*, 3rd edition, page 522.

9. Ibid., page 325.

10. Dyer, Dr. Wayne W. *Inspiration: Your Ultimate Calling*, page 5.

11. Kabat-Zinn, Jon. *Full Catastrophe Living*, page 443.

Works Cited/Bibliography

The American Heritage College Dictionary, 3rd edition. Houghton Mifflin Company, 1997.

Cameron, Julia. *The Artist's Way: A Spiritual Path to Higher Creativity*. New York: Penguin Putnam, Inc., 2002.

Dyer, Dr. Wayne W. *Inspiration: Your Ultimate Calling*. Carlsbad, CA: Hay House, Inc., 2006.

Eker, T. Harv. *Secrets of the Millionaire Mind: Mastering the Inner Game Of Wealth*. New York: Harper Collins, 2005.

Olsen, Kristin Gottschalk. *The Encyclopedia of Alternative Health Care*. New York: Simon and Schuster, 1989.

Ford, Debbie. *The Dark Side of the Light Chasers: Reclaiming Your Power, Creativity, Brilliance, And Dreams*. New York: Riverhead Books, 1998.

Kabat-Zinn, Jon. *Full Catastrophe Living*. New York: Dell Publishing, 1990.

Katie, Byron. *Loving What Is: Four Questions That Can Change Your Life*. New York: Harmony Books, 2002.

Kelley, Sheila. *The S Factor: Strip Workouts of Every Woman*. New York: Workman Publishing, 2003.

Kingston, Karen. *Clear Your Clutter with Feng Shui*. New York: Random House, 1999.

Norris, Gunilla. *Inviting Silence*. New York: Blueridge, 2004.

Northrup, Christiane. *Women's Bodies, Women's Wisdom: Creating Physical and Emotional Health and Healing.* New York: Bantam Books, 1998.

Roman, Sanaya and Duane Packer. *Creating Money: Keys To Abundance.* Tiburon, CA: HJ Kramer, 1988.

Rosenberg, Marshall. *Nonviolent Communication: A Language of Life.* Encinitas, CA: Puddle Dancer Press, 2003.

Roth, Geneen. *When Food is Love: Exploring The Relationship Between Eating And Intimacy.* New York, NY: Plume, 1992.

Roth, Geneen. *When You Eat at the Refrigerator, Pull Up A Chair: 50 Ways To Feel Thin, Gorgeous, and Happy (When You Feel Anything But).* New York: Hyperion, 1998.

Ruiz, Miguel. *The Four Agreements.* San Rafael, CA: Amber-Allen Publishing, 1997.

Thakor, Manisha and Sharon Kedar. *On My Own Two Feet: A Modern Girl's Guide To Personal Finance.* Avon, MA: F+W Publications Company, 2007.

Tolle, Eckhart. *The Power Of Now: A Guide to Spiritual Enlightenment.* Vancouver, Canada: Namaste Publishing, 1999.

Walsh, Peter. *It's All Too Much: An Easy Plan For Living A Richer Life With Less Stuff.* New York: Free Press, 2007.

Zukav, Gary. *The Seat of the Soul.* New York: Fireside / Simon & Schuster, 1990.